A NEW INTRODUCTION

Stories of the Early Church

R H HORTON · REDVERS BRANDLING

Illustrated by Juliette Palmer

Hodder & Stoughton

A MEMBER OF THE HODDER HEADLINE GROUP

British Library Cataloguing in Publication Data

A catalogue for this book is
available from the British Library

ISBN 0 340 52356 5
First published 1963
Second Edition 1990

Impression number   10 9 8 7 6 5 4 3
Year   1998 1997 1996 1995

Copyright © 1963 Robert H Horton
Copyright © 1990 Redvers Brandling

All rights reserved. No part of this publication may be
reproduced or transmitted in any form or by any means,
electronic or mechanical, including photocopy, recording,
or any information storage and retrieval system, without
permission in writing from the publisher or under licence
from the Copyright Licensing Agency Limited. Further
details of such licences (for reprographic reproduction) may
be obtained from the Copyright Licensing Agency Limited,
of 90 Tottenham Court Road, London W1P 9HE.

Typeset by Taurus Graphics, Abingdon
Printed in Hong Kong for Hodder & Stoughton
Educational, a division of Hodder Headline Plc,
338 Euston Road, London NW1 3BH by Colorcraft Ltd.

Preface

This series, *A New Introduction to the Bible*, is made up of four books and four accompanying blackline master workpacks.
It has been written for the 9–13 age range and forms a complete Religious Education resource at this level.

The stories in the four books have been taken from Robert Horton's series *An Introduction to the Bible*. These stories have not been altered in any way because they still 'satisfy a pressing need for a simple and straightforward account of the Bible story, told in a language which can be readily understood'.

New question sections have been written by Redvers Brandling and these are set at the end of each story and labelled 'Your turn now . . .' They have been carefully written with modern thinking about assessment and assessment techniques clearly in mind so that they not only test knowledge and comprehension, but also fit into the wider context of whole curriculum planning.

The workpacks which accompany the four books, one pack per book, further support the work begun in the 'Your turn now . . .' sections. There is one worksheet per story and the work set here is widely varied in order to develop as many skills as possible. The range of tasks includes Cloze procedure, crosswords, wordsearches, all forms of creative and formal writing exercises, and visual/artwork exercises such as enlarging pictures and illustrating text.

The books and packs have been carefully designed for ease of use and are fully illustrated throughout. In the case of the books the ever-popular illustrations drawn for Horton's series have been retained because of their suitability as artwork resource material. As a series *A New Introduction to the Bible* forms a complete course of work which is appropriate for use with pupils of all abilities and from all religious backgrounds.

Contents

CHAP.		PAGE
1	The Twelve Apostles	7
2	The Day of Pentecost	9
3	The Healing of a Lame Man	11
4	Peter and John in Prison	13
5	The Church begins to Grow	15
6	Peter and John escape from Prison	17
7	The Death of Stephen	20
8	Philip and the Man from Ethiopia	22
9	On the Road to Damascus	24
10	Saul escapes from Damascus	26
11	Peter performs Two Miracles	29
12	Peter and the Centurion	31
13	Peter is saved from King Herod	33
14	Paul and Barnabas, the First Missionaries	36
15	The Stoning of Paul	38
16	Paul sets out for Europe	40
17	Paul and Silas in Prison	43
18	The Unknown God	46
19	A Riot at Ephesus	48
20	Paul heals a Boy	50
21	Paul meets his Enemies in the Temple	53
22	Paul in a Roman Prison	55
23	Paul on Trial	58
24	The Voyage to Rome	60
25	The Shipwreck	62

26	Paul's Last Days in Rome	64
27	Christian Behaviour	67
28	Christian Love	69
29	The Christian's Armour	71
30	Christian Faith	74
31	Christian Hope	76
32	Christian Friendship	78
	Dates of Events and the Books of the New Testament	80

— I —
The Twelve Apostles

We can read about the early Christian Church in the fifth book of the New Testament. This book is called the Acts of the Apostles. It was written by Luke, who also wrote one of the Gospels. Luke was not a Jew but a Gentile. The name Gentile was given by the Jews to anyone who was not a Jew. We shall find Luke's name when we read the stories of Paul's missionary journeys, for he was a friend of Paul.

Our story of the early Church begins with the Ascension of Jesus into heaven. During the forty days after he rose from the dead Jesus appeared to his disciples many times. The disciples had to get used to the idea that Jesus was no longer with them in the same way as before. Then he had been there to talk with

Jesus ascends into heaven.

them and to help them. Now they had to learn how to carry on when he was not with them. They were able to carry on because they knew that his spirit was with them.

On that great day when the disciples saw Jesus for the last time, they saw him ascend into heaven. But before he left them he told them what they must do. They must wait in Jerusalem until God sent them the power of his Holy Spirit. Then they must go out and preach to the people in Jerusalem, in Judea, in Samaria, and even in other lands.

When the disciples came back to Jerusalem they went to the Upper Room. This was the room where they had eaten the Last Supper with Jesus, the night of his arrest. Now there were eleven disciples in the room: Judas was dead. Mary, the mother of Jesus, and other men and women were there with them.

These men and women were not called Christians yet. But they were really the first members of the Christian Church. Altogether there were more than one hundred of them. Their leader was Peter, and he told them that they must find a man to take the place of Judas. Then there would be twelve of them again.

Among the men who had been with them from the start of Jesus' ministry they found only two. Then they prayed to God to show them which one was to take Judas's place. Matthias (*Math-eye-ass*) was chosen to make up the twelve.

From this time we call the disciples 'Apostles'. No longer are they learners, but teachers.

Your turn now...

Research and discussion

Read verses 6–14 of Acts, Chapter 1. Then with your friends and teacher discuss the following.
a) What did Jesus promise his disciples?
b) What were the instructions given to the disciples?
c) How many disciples were present in the Upper Room?
d) Who were they?

Writing

1 Write down the meaning of the following words. Use a dictionary where necessary:
   Gentile   disciple   apostle.

2 Read Acts, Chapter I until you find the verse in which Jesus told the disciples what they must do. Write this verse out.

Drama

With some friends act out the scene in the Upper Room.

— 2 —
The Day of Pentecost

Pentecost was a great harvest festival of the Jews. It was to be a great day for the early Christians, too. Today we call this day Whitsunday.

On the day of Pentecost the apostles were all in the Upper Room when a strange thing happened. First came the sound of a great wind in the room. Then they saw what looked like flames touching each one of them. Often in the old days of the Jewish people, God had come to them in the wind and the fire. Now he had come again. They had waited, as Jesus had told them, and God had sent his Holy Spirit to them.

Map of Jerusalem and surrounding countries.

Full of joy the apostles went out into the streets to preach. As they spoke all the people were amazed. There were people of all kinds, from many different lands. Yet each was able to hear the apostles speak in the words of his own land.

Some of those who stood by said that the apostles must be drunk. Then Peter stood up and spoke to the crowd.

'How can they be drunk so early in the day?' Peter asked. 'It is only nine o'clock! No, this is what the prophet Joel (*Jo-ell*) said would happen. God has sent his Holy Spirit to us, who are his servants.'

Then Peter went on to tell them all about Jesus, how he had been killed and had risen again from the dead. When they heard Peter's words many of the people were ashamed.

'What must we do?' they asked.

'You must repent,' said Peter, 'and be baptised.'

That day hundreds of people were baptised and became followers of Jesus. The apostles did many great miracles. The new 'Christians' gave up their houses and their money and shared them with one another.

Each day they met for prayer. They ate the bread and drank the wine as Jesus, at the Last Supper, had said they must. And each day more and more people joined the apostles as followers of Jesus.

Your turn now...

Research and writing

1 Read Acts, Chapter 2, verses 1–4. Now imagine you were an apostle in the Upper Room. Describe what happened to you.

2 Write down the meaning of the following words. Use a dictionary where necessary:
   Pentecost   repent   baptised

Drama

Act out with some friends the scene where Peter speaks to the crowd.

OR

Draw the scene, putting the words spoken in speech bubbles.

Note
Write in your book: PENTECOST – WHITSUNDAY. Pentecost is a Greek word for fiftieth. Pentecost was fifty days after the Passover.

— 3 —

The Healing of a Lame Man

One day Peter and John were going to the Temple to pray. They were now members of the early Christian Church, but they were still good Jews. It was three o'clock, the hour of prayer at the Temple.

They approached one of the main gates into the Temple. It

Peter told the man to look up.

was called the Beautiful Gate and, as its name tells us, it was very beautiful. Every day a lame man was put down near this gate by his friends. He had never been able to walk, or even to stand. He could not work. So he was carried to this spot to beg from the people who went in and out of the Temple.

When the lame man saw Peter and John he held out his hand to beg from them. The two apostles stopped and Peter told the man to look up at them. He did this, hoping that they were going to give him some coins. But Peter spoke some wonderful words to him:

'I have no money, no silver or gold, but I will give you what I have. In the name of Jesus, get up and walk!'

These were strange words to a man who had never been able to walk in his life. Yet, as Peter took him by the hand, the lame man felt new strength come to him. He stood up. Then he began to walk, to jump, and to run. In his joy he shouted out his praise to God for what had been done.

As the man held on to Peter and John people ran to him from all parts of the Temple. They had heard the shouts and they were amazed by what they saw. All of them knew the man, for they had seen him, day after day, as he sat at the Beautiful Gate to beg. They stared at the man, and at Peter and John.

'Don't look at us,' said Peter. 'This is not our work. It is the power of Jesus that has healed this man, Jesus, whom you put to death.'

Then Peter went on to speak bravely to the people. He told them how they had helped to kill Jesus. Then he told them how Jesus had risen from the dead. And now, in front of them all, the power of Jesus had made the lame man well and strong.

Your turn now...

Research and discussion

Discuss the following with your friends and teacher:
Being lame or disabled in any way is not easy. How do you think our society copes with such problems?

Writing

The following words are all used in this chapter. Put each of them into a sentence to show what they mean:
Temple   amazed   miracle

> **Drama**
>
> With some of your friends act out this story from the lame man's point of view. Use Peter's words to him in your drama.
>
> Try to capture the atmosphere of the occasion by both words and actions.

4

Peter and John in Prison

After the healing of the lame man in the Temple, Peter went on to speak to the people about Jesus. As he did so some of the priests and rulers of the Temple came up. They were very angry when they heard the name of Jesus. When they had killed Jesus they hoped they had heard the last of him. Now his name was being used again, in the Temple. Peter and John were arrested at once.

By this time it was evening. It was too late to try the apostles that day. They were put into the prison for the night. But many of the people who had seen the lame man healed and who had heard the words of Peter now became followers of Jesus.

Next day the High Priest and the Council met to try Peter and John. The two apostles stood before the Sadducees (*Sad-you-sees*), the Pharisees (*Farry-sees*) and the Scribes. The Sadducees were the rich priests; the Pharisees were the leaders of the Jewish religion; the Scribes were the lawyers and the teachers of the Law. Then the two men were asked to say how they had healed the lame man. When Peter spoke it seemed that he was filled with the power of God.

'You ask us how this man was healed,' said Peter. 'Jesus whom you killed and whom God raised to life again – he has healed this man who stands here with us now.'

The Council saw how bold the apostles were. They knew that a great miracle had been done on the lame man. Hundreds of people in the city of Jerusalem had seen it happen. But the Council had made up their mind that the name of Jesus must not be spoken again in Jerusalem.

'You must not speak at all, or teach, in the name of Jesus,' the apostles were told.

'Must we listen to you,' asked Peter and John, 'or to God? We

Peter and John were arrested.

must say and do only what God tells us.'

The High Priest and the Council were very angry, but there was nothing to be done. Again they told the apostles that they must not use the name of Jesus and then they let them go free.

Your turn now...

Research and writing

Read Acts, Chapter 4, verses 1–10. Now answer the following questions in sentences.

a) Why were the priests and rulers of the Temple angry when Jesus was mentioned?

b) How many followers of Jesus were there at this time?
c) Which leaders of the people were present at the trial of Peter and John?
d) How did Peter say the lame man had been healed?
e) Who were the Sadducees, the Pharisees and the Scribes?

Discussion

Discuss the following points with your friends and teacher.
a) Do you think the priests and rulers of the Temple were right to arrest Peter and John?
b) Why do you think Peter answered so boldly?
c) Why did the Council forbid the name of Jesus to be spoken?

5

The Church begins to Grow

After Peter and John had been set free they went back to tell the others what had been done. Then they went out into the city to preach to the people. Many more men and women became followers of Jesus. They still went to the Temple at the time of prayer and to the synagogue on the Sabbath day. But they also met as 'Christians'. They had no church to go to. Many of them met in the Upper Room in the house of John Mark's mother. (We shall read more about John Mark when we come to the stories about Paul.) Some met in other houses. When they had meals together and 'broke bread' they remembered the Last Supper. They thought of the words of Jesus when he had told them to do this in memory of him.

The new members of the Church began to share all that they had. People who had a house or land sold it and brought the money to the apostles. This money was used to help those who were poor and in need. One man who sold his field and gave the money to the apostles was named Joseph Barnabas, a man who had come from the island of Cyprus. He was to go with Paul on his first missionary journey, and we shall read about him later on in this book.

There is a sad story about one man and his wife who sold what they had. But when they came to the apostles with the

Some of the sick were laid in the street.

money they agreed to keep some of it back. There was no rule that they must give up their money. But they did wrong when they tried to make Peter think that they had given all. They were pretending to be good, but they were telling lies, not only to Peter, but also to God. The story is sad because both the man and his wife died. What a lesson this was for the apostles and their friends.

Still the Church grew. Many people came to hear the words of the apostles as they spoke in the streets of Jerusalem and in the Temple. Crowds of them joined the followers of Jesus. Many miracles were done by the apostles. People from Jerusalem and from all the neighbouring towns brought the sick to be healed. Some were even laid on beds in the street so that Peter's shadow fell on them when he passed by. All who came were healed by the power of Jesus.

Your turn now...

Research and writing

Read Acts, Chapter 5, verses 1 – 11 and then answer the following questions in sentences.

a) What were the names of the two people who sold their possessions?
b) What did they do with the money from the sale?
c) Why was Peter sad about them?
d) What happened to them?
e) What effect did this story have on the others?

Discussion

Discuss the following with your friends and teacher:

We all have possessions. Would you be prepared to part with yours for some cause? How do you think the new members of the church felt when they had parted with their possessions?

Drama

Mime the sick people waiting for Peter to pass by and heal them.

6

Peter and John escape from Prison

News soon spread in Jerusalem about the work of the apostles and the healing of the sick. The priests were very angry when they heard that these men had not obeyed their orders. They were still preaching about Jesus and healing people by his power.

The High Priest sent his men to arrest the apostles. This was done and they were put into the prison for the night. But during the night a wonderful thing happened. The cell was filled with light and God's angel was there. He led the apostles out of their cell.

'Go to the Temple,' the angel said, 'and speak to the people the word of God.'

Early in the morning the apostles went to the Temple and

The soldiers found the cell empty.

stood in the courtyard. There they spoke to the people about Jesus.

About this time the High Priest called the Council together and sent for the prisoners. When the men who had been sent came to the cell they found it empty. They did not know what to think, so they came back to the Council.

'We found the prison locked,' they said, 'and the warders were standing at the door of the cell. But when we went in to bring out the prisoners, the cell was empty.'

The priests were amazed at what they heard. They began to wonder what would happen next. As they were talking a man came in from the Temple courtyard.

'Those men whom you put into prison are in the Temple,' he said. 'They are teaching the people about Jesus.'

Some Temple soldiers were sent to bring the apostles to the

High Priest. The captain was very careful not to use any violence. He was afraid that the crowd might stone him and his men. So he brought the apostles quietly to the Council room. They stood before the High Priest.

'We have told you that you must not teach in the name of Jesus,' said the High Priest. 'All the people in the city hear what you say. They hear how you blame us for the death of this Jesus.'

'We have to obey God rather than you,' said Peter. 'We must do what he tells us.'

When they heard this the priests were very angry. Many of them wanted to put the apostles to death. But there was one Pharisee who stood up and spoke to them. His name was Gamaliel (*Ga-may-li-el*). He sent the apostles out of the room.

'Be careful what you do,' he told the Council. 'Leave these men alone. If God is not with them their work will soon be forgotten. But if God is on their side you can do nothing. You might even find yourselves fighting against God himself.'

The Council agreed with these words and sent for the apostles. They beat them and once more they warned them that they must not use the name of Jesus. The apostles were glad to think that they had been able to suffer for Jesus, who had suffered and died for them.

So they went out into the Temple again. There, in the Temple, in houses, and in the streets, they went on teaching the people about Jesus.

Your turn now...

Research and writing

Answer the following questions in sentences.
a) What were the apostles doing which made the priests angry?
b) What feelings did the priests have towards the apostles?
c) Why were the prisoners no longer in the cell?
d) How did the captain bring the apostles to the Council room?
e) What was Peter's reply to the High Priest?

Discussion

Discuss the following with your friends and teacher.
a) Why do you think the priests feared the apostles?
b) What was Gamaliel's advice? Do you agree with it?

c) Do you think the priests' treatment of the apostles was effective?

Illustration

Draw (or act) the scene where the apostles are in the Council room before the High Priest.

— 7 —

The Death of Stephen

As more and more people joined the early Church there was much work for the apostles to do. There were many poor people to be looked after. The apostles did not want this work to stop their teaching so they called the disciples together. They told them to choose seven good men for the work of looking after the poor and needy.

One of these seven men was Stephen. He was a wise man, filled with the power of God. He had done many wonderful things for the people. But he was soon to get into trouble. Some of the enemies of the apostles began to argue with him, and to accuse him of speaking against the Law and against God.

The priests and scribes were very angry when they heard this. Stephen was arrested and brought before the High Priest and the Council. Some men were bribed to tell lies about him, just as men had done at the trial of Jesus himself.

'This man keeps speaking against the holy Temple and against the Law,' said these witnesses.

Stephen stood there, quite unafraid, as the High Priest asked him if this was true. It was a very serious matter. The Jews were jealous of their Temple and Law. They thought of the Temple as the home of God, the one place where he could be worshipped truly.

Then Stephen spoke. He told them that there was no place, not even the Temple, that could be called the home of God. God spoke to men in all kinds of places. Then he showed them how they had failed God as his chosen people. Right from the early days God had often been forgotten. His messengers, the

Stephen was stoned to death.

prophets, had been ill-treated.

'Your fathers ill-treated and killed God's prophets,' said Stephen, 'men who told you about the coming of the Christ. Now you have killed the Christ himself.'

These words enraged the members of the Council. They took hold of Stephen and hurried him out of the city. There they stoned him to death, while a man named Saul looked after their cloaks. We shall be reading a great deal more about this man Saul later in this book.

So Stephen died, praying that Jesus would forgive his enemies for what they had done.

Your turn now...

Research and writing

Answer the following in sentences.
a) Why did the apostles need to recruit more men?
b) Describe Stephen's character in your own words.
c) Why were the members of the Council angry with Stephen?

Discussion

1 With your friends and teacher discuss the story and fate of Stephen. Here are some words to help you: dangerous – blasphemy – brave – merciful – violent. Use a dictionary if necessary.

2 Read Acts, Chapter 7, verses 58–60. What reminds you of the death of Jesus here?

— 8 —

Philip and the Man from Ethiopia

After the death of Stephen the enemies of the disciples often ill-treated the members of the early Church. Many followers of Jesus left Jerusalem and went to other towns, some of them to other lands. But wherever they went the word of God went with them. By trying to stop the growth of the Christian Church, its enemies only helped it to spread more and more.

About this time a man named Philip went to preach in the city of Samaria. This was not the disciple of Jesus who was called Philip. As Stephen had been, he was one of the seven men chosen to work among the poor and needy people of Jerusalem.

The people of Samaria were not very friendly with the Jews, but they gladly listened to what Philip had to say. Many sick people were healed by him, and many men and women were baptised in the name of Jesus. When the apostles at Jerusalem heard of these great events in Samaria they sent Peter and John to preach there and to pray for the coming of God's Spirit to these people.

Philip himself was called away by God. There was work for him to do in other places. God sent him to the road that led from Jerusalem through the desert to Gaza (*Gay-za*) and then on into

Philip sat in the chariot and told him about Jesus.

Egypt.

Along this road a great man was riding in his chariot. He was the treasurer of Candace (*Can-da-see*), Queen of Ethiopia. He had been up to Jerusalem to worship God, and now he was on his way home. As he sat there he was reading from the book of the prophet Isaiah (*Eyes-eye-a*). At once Philip, led by God, ran up to him.

'Do you understand what you are reading?' asked Philip.

'I cannot understand, unless someone explains to me,' the man replied.

Then he asked Philip to come up into the chariot and sit with him. Philip began to tell the man all about Jesus, and how he was the Christ about whom the prophet Isaiah had spoken. As they went along they came to some water by the side of the road.

'See, here is water,' said the man. 'Is there any reason why I should not be baptised?'

He stopped the chariot and, with Philip, went into the water and was baptised. Then he got into his chariot again and set off for his home, full of joy at what had happened. But Philip went off to do the work of God in other places.

Your turn now...

Research and writing

Answer these questions in sentences.
a) Which city did Philip visit?
b) What did he do there?
c) How did the people receive him?

Discussion

Read Acts, Chapter 8, verses 32–33. With your friends and teacher discuss the meaning of the words that the Ethiopian was reading.

Drama

Prepare a detailed mime of the full story of Philip and the Ethiopian. Try and capture the atmosphere by clear movements and expressions.

— 9 —

On the Road to Damascus

In Chapter 7 we heard of a man named Saul. It was he who looked after the cloaks of the men who stoned Stephen to death. Now he and his friends began to persecute the followers of Jesus in Jerusalem. Many of them were arrested and put into prison. Many others fled from the city to places where they could be safe.

But the Christians had now spread far from Jerusalem, to other towns and villages, and even to other lands. Small groups met together in the name of Jesus. Even in Damascus, many miles away in Syria, these men and women were meeting together.

Saul had made up his mind to stop the growth of the new

Saul was blinded by a light from heaven.

Church. He asked the High Priest if he could go to Damascus and arrest any men or women who were followers of 'the Way'. The early Christians were often called by this name, the Way meaning the Way of Life, or the Way of Christ.

It was on the road to Damascus that Saul's life was suddenly changed. As he and his men came near to the city a dazzling light shone round about him, far brighter than the sun. Saul was blinded by this light from heaven. He fell down with his face to the ground. Then he heard a voice speaking to him:

'Saul, Saul, why do you persecute me?'

'Who are you, Lord?' said Saul, looking up.

'I am Jesus, whom you are persecuting,' was the answer.

Then Saul saw the shining figure of the risen Jesus before him. This was a sight he never forgot. Often in the days to follow he spoke of his meeting with Jesus, face to face, on the road to Damascus.

Jesus told Saul that he must go into the city, and there he would be told what to do. The men who were with Saul stood there, silent and afraid. They had heard the voice but they saw no one.

Saul rose from the ground, but he could see nothing. He was blind. He had come to Damascus as the proud enemy of the Christian Church. But he went into the city a blind man, led by his friends. For three days he was blind and had nothing to eat or drink.

Your turn now...

Research and writing

Read Acts, Chapter 8, verses 1–13 and Acts, Chapter 9, verses 1–2.
a) Write down a list of words which you think could be used to describe the character of Saul.
b) What were the early Christians often called?

Discussion

Discuss with your friends and teacher why the persecution of the early Christians failed.
   Try to think of some other situations where persecution has failed.

Writing

In your own words tell how Saul met Jesus on the road to Damascus.

— 10 —

Saul escapes from Damascus

In Damascus there lived a good man named Ananias (*An-an-eye-as*). He was a follower of Jesus and one day Jesus spoke to him in a vision.

'Go to the street that is named Straight,' said Jesus. 'Ask at the house of Judas for a man named Saul. In a vision Saul has

Saul was let down in a basket.

seen you coming to him to heal his blindness.'

Ananias did not want to go to Saul. He had heard a great deal about this man. He knew of all the evil that he had done to the early Church in Jerusalem. He knew, too, that Saul had come to Damascus to arrest all the followers of Jesus in his city.

'Go to him,' said Jesus. 'I have chosen this man to preach my name to all people.'

So Ananias went to the house of Judas and found Saul. He told Saul how Jesus had sent him to give him back his sight. All at once Saul's eyes were opened and he could see again. He was baptised. Then, for the first time since he had come to the city, he had some food to make him stronger.

For some days he stayed with the disciples in Damascus. He was a new man. Instead of being an enemy of the Church he began to preach in the Jewish synagogues. Everywhere he went he told the people that Jesus was the Son of God. All who heard him and knew why he had come to Damascus were amazed at the change in Saul.

But the men who had come to Damascus with Saul, and their friends in the city, were very angry. They began to plot against Saul and made up their minds to kill him. So that Saul could not escape they kept watch on the city gates by day and by night. But Saul found out about this plot. One night the disciples took him to the city wall. Then, very quietly, they let him down in a basket on the end of ropes.

So Saul escaped and went back to Jerusalem. When he tried to join with the disciples there they were afraid of him, and did not trust him. But Barnabas told them how Saul had met the Lord Jesus and spoken with him on the way to Damascus. He told them how Saul had boldly preached about Jesus in the city.

At last Saul became one of them and went about Jerusalem and the towns round about preaching and teaching about Jesus. Here, too, plots were made against Saul by his former friends. So the disciples sent him away to Caesarea, and from there to Tarsus, where he could be safe.

Your turn now...

Research and writing

1. a) In your own words write down the reason why Ananias did not want to visit Saul.
   b) What was the outcome of his visit?

2. Complete each of the following sentences with what you think are the most suitable words.
   a) Saul escaped from Damascus by _____ .
   b) Barnabas was _____ .
   c) Tarsus was _____ .

Illustration

Draw the scene between Ananias and Saul. Pay careful attention to drawing both. Try to make the background accurate. Try to show in your picture the atmosphere of the occasion.

11

Peter performs Two Miracles

For a time we shall leave Saul and return to the other disciples. The early Church had kept on growing and had spread in Judea and Galilee and Samaria. The disciples went from town to town, preaching and teaching about Jesus.

One day Peter came to the town of Lydda (*Lidd-a*). Here lived a man by the name of Aeneas (*Ee-knee-ass*). He was paralysed, and for eight long years he had lain in bed. Then Peter came to his house, and entered the room where the sick man lay.

'Aeneas,' said Peter to him, 'Jesus Christ has healed you. Get up and make your bed.'

At once Aeneas rose from his bed and was well again. The news soon spread in the town and many people became followers of Jesus.

Not very far from Lydda, on the sea coast, was the town of Joppa. Here lived a disciple named Tabitha. She was a very

Map showing places mentioned in the early days of the Church.

kind woman, doing all that she could to help the poor and needy. But while Peter was in Lydda, Tabitha died. The disciples sent word to Peter, asking him to come at once, for Tabitha was dead.

Peter hurried to Joppa and came to Tabitha's house. At once he went to the room where the dead woman was lying. Many women stood around her, weeping. They held the clothes that Tabitha had made and given to them while she was alive. Peter sent them all out of the room. Then he knelt down and prayed. After this he turned to the dead woman and spoke.

'Tabitha, get up,' he said.

The dead woman opened her eyes and when she saw Peter she sat up. Peter took her by the hand and called back the others to the room to see her alive and well. Once more the news spread around, and many of the people of Joppa became followers of Jesus.

Your turn now...

Research and writing

Imagine you were an eye-witness at the healing of Aeneas. Write an account of what you saw. The following words might give you some ideas: helpless – amazement – miracle.

Illustration

Using the passage to help you, draw a picture of the scene at Tabitha's house when Peter spoke to her. Write his words by your picture.

Discussion

With your friends and teacher discuss the following:
    What effect did Peter's miracles at Lydda and Joppa have on the people of these towns?

Note
Joppa is now called Jaffa. What food do we eat that comes from Jaffa?

12
Peter and the Centurion

In the town of Caesarea (*Seas-a-ree-a*) there lived a centurion named Cornelius (*Corn-eel-i-us*). He was a good man and he and his family believed in God. He spent much time in prayer and gave money to those who were poor and in need.

One day Cornelius had a vision in which he saw an angel of God. The angel told him that God had heard his prayers and seen his kindness. Then he went on:

'Send some of your men to Joppa, to find a man named Peter. He is at the house of Simon the tanner, by the seaside. Tell them to bring Peter here to you.'

At once Cornelius called three of his men and sent them off to Joppa.

About noon the next day, while these men were on their way, Peter was on the roof of his house, praying to God. He was very hungry and fell asleep. Then he had a strange dream. He saw what seemed to be a great sheet coming down from heaven. In it were all kinds of animals and birds. Then a voice spoke to him:

'Get up, Peter! Kill and eat.'

'I have never eaten anything that is common or unclean,' said Peter. (The Jewish Law did not allow Jews to eat the flesh of some animals, such as the pig, which was called unclean.)

Again Peter heard the voice, telling him that he must not call things unclean that God had made. Three times this was done, and then the sheet was drawn up to heaven again.

Peter did not know what this dream meant. As he wondered, the men sent by Cornelius came to the gate, asking for him. Peter heard God telling him that he must go with them for he, God, had sent them to him.

The next day Peter and some friends set off with the men, and a day later they came to Caesarea. Cornelius, who was waiting for him, was full of joy when he saw Peter. He fell at his feet as if to worship him.

'Get up,' said Peter, 'you must not do that. I am only a man like yourself.'

When Peter went into the house he found many people there, waiting to hear his words. Then Peter knew what his vision had meant. Jews were not allowed by the Law to mix with foreign people, for they were 'unclean'. But God had shown him that all

In the great sheet were all kinds of animals and birds.

people were his people. He must not call any man unclean.

So Peter spoke to the people there about Jesus. Even as he spoke God's Spirit came to them all. The Jews were amazed that this should happen to Gentiles (foreigners). They were taken outside and there Peter baptised them all in the name of Jesus.

This is a very important story, as these were the first Gentiles to be baptised by Peter as members of the early Church. Peter had learnt that he must now preach, not only to Jews, but to all people.

Your turn now...

Research and writing

1 Some of the following sentences are not true. Write out in your books only the ones which are correct.
   a) The centurion was called Caesarea.
   b) Cornelius was a devout man who helped the poor and the needy.
   c) Cornelius sent out four of his servants to bring Peter to his house.

2 Put the following words into sentences to show their meaning: foreign   acceptable   respect.

Discussion

Discuss with your friends and teacher Peter's dream and how he came to realise its true meaning.

13

Peter is Saved from King Herod

The apostles and the other disciples in Jerusalem soon heard what Peter had done in the house of Cornelius at Caesarea. They asked him why he had gone into the house of a man who was not a Jew and why he had eaten with Gentiles. Peter told them all about his vision of the sheet with its birds and animals, and how God had taught him a lesson.

When they had heard this story the apostles knew that Jesus was calling Gentiles, as well as Jews, to be his followers. Already Philip and Peter had preached to Gentiles and baptised them. Now other leaders of the early Church went out to do the same.

About this time was the Feast of the Passover. King Herod tried to please the Jewish leaders by ill-treating some of the well-known members of the early Church. He took the apostle James, the brother of John and one of Jesus' twelve disciples, and put him to death. Then he took Peter and had him put into prison. There he was closely guarded by soldiers.

While Peter was in prison all his friends prayed to God for his safety. The time drew near when Herod was going to deal with Peter, probably to kill him. The night before, Peter was asleep in his cell. On each side he was chained to a soldier. Outside the door other guards were on duty.

Then a wonderful thing happened. The whole cell shone with a bright light and an angel touched Peter, waking him up. He told Peter to get up and at once his chains fell away from his arms.

'Put on your coat and your sandals,' said the angel, 'and follow me.'

Peter did what he was told as if in a dream. In fact he did not realise that all this was really happening – he thought that he was seeing a vision. But they passed the door of the cell, then other doors. At last they came to the iron gate of the prison. Outside was the dark, open street. This gate seemed to open by itself and they went through. Then the angel left Peter.

Now Peter knew that he was free. God had sent his angel to

The prison gate seemed to open by itself.

save him from Herod and the Jews. He went off to the house of Mary, mother of John Mark. This was the house of the Last Supper, and was now a meeting place for disciples. In the house at that very moment many people had met to pray for Peter.

Peter knocked at the door and a maid came to see who was there. When she heard the voice she knew that it was Peter. In her great joy and excitement she forgot to open the door, but ran to tell those inside. The others did not believe her. When she said that it was true they thought that Peter must have been put to death and that this was his spirit.

Peter kept on knocking. At last the door was opened. Those inside were amazed to see Peter really standing there, safe and well. He told them what had happened and then, as he knew that a search would soon be made for him, Peter went to a safer place.

Your turn now...

Research and writing

1 Check on the facts and then answer the following in sentences.
   a) Which Feast was being celebrated in this chapter?
   b) Why was James put to death?
   c) Why were apostles and other disciples puzzled by Peter's actions at Caesarea?
   d) What did Herod do to Peter?

2 Read Acts, Chapter 12, verses 6–10.
Next, either write your own description of Peter's imprisonment and escape.

OR

Draw a sequence of pictures starting with his imprisonment and ending with his knocking on Mary's door. Put captions under each picture.

Research and discussion

With your friends and teacher discuss what happened when Peter's escape was discovered. What kind of man do you think Herod was? Compare punishments then with modern-day methods.

14

Paul and Barnabus, the First Missionaries

The map in Chapter 11 shows a city named Antioch (*Anti-ok*). When the Jews began to persecute the early followers of Jesus, Antioch became a great centre of the Christian Church. It was here that the name Christian was first used. The Gentiles who were not Christians heard the followers of Jesus preaching.
They kept using the word 'Christ' when they spoke of him. Soon the Gentiles began to speak of them as 'Christians', a name that has been used ever since. And it was from Antioch that the first missionaries were sent out to other lands.

God spoke to the leaders of the Church at Antioch and told them that he had special work for Barnabas and Saul to do. This work was to go and preach to the Jews who lived in other lands. From this time Saul was known by his Greek name, Paul.

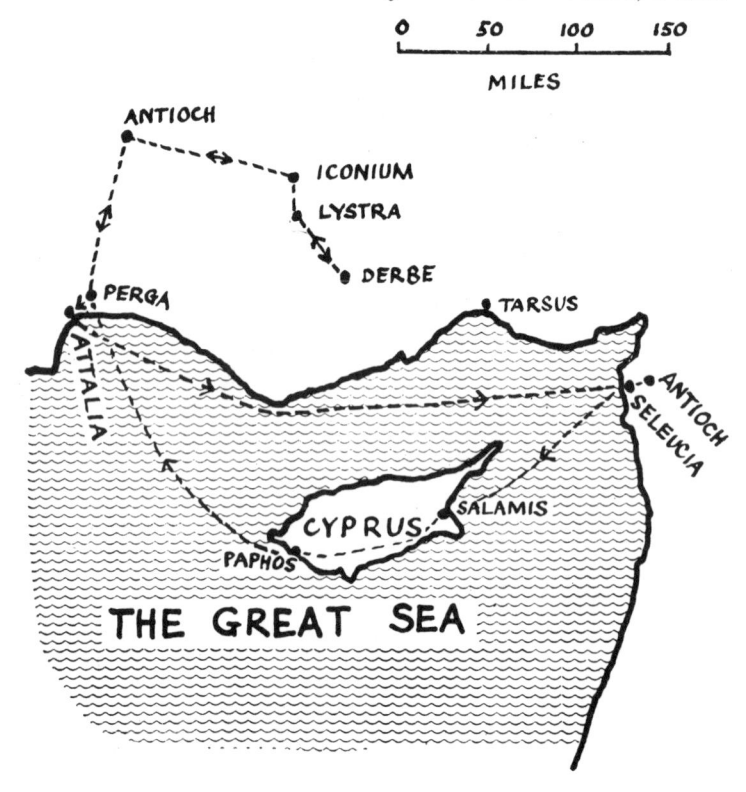

Map of Paul's first missionary journey.

The two men went down to the sea and sailed to the island of Cyprus (*Sigh-pruss*). Barnabas was well known here and had many friends among the people. With them went John Mark, a young man from Jerusalem. We think that he lived at the house with the Upper Room, and Barnabas was his uncle.

When Paul and Barnabas landed on Cyprus they went from one end of the island to the other. The people they met believed in magic and the apostles found it hard to drive out the magic and teach them the word of God. At last they came to the town of Paphos (*Pay-foss*) and met the ruler of the island.

They talked to the ruler about Jesus, but his magician, a man named Elymas (*Elly-mass*), was angry. He did not want his master to turn to a new faith. So he spoke out against the words of Paul and Barnabas. Then Paul turned to him.

'You are an evil man,' he said. 'You are trying to stop the true word of Jesus. He will punish you, and you will be blind for a time.'

As soon as Paul had said these words Elymas was struck blind and had to be led away by his friends. The ruler, when he saw this, believed in what Paul had told him about Jesus.

From Cyprus Paul and his friends sailed across to the mainland and came to Perga. It was here that John Mark left them and went home to Jerusalem. He was only young, and perhaps he was not yet ready for the hard work to be done. He may have been afraid, too, for the work was sometimes dangerous.

Your turn now...

Research and writing

Imagine you are Paul and write your diary for this period.

Investigation

Look at the map and the scale. Now work out how far Paul and Barnabas travelled.

Drama

With some friends mime or act the story of Paul and how he met the ruler of Paphos, and Elymas.
   Try to capture the atmosphere of these events in your drama.

15

The Stoning of Paul

After John Mark had left them at Perga, Paul and Barnabas went off to the north. They came to another town with the name of Antioch. This was not, of course, the Antioch from which their journey had begun. Here, one Sabbath, they were asked to speak in the Jewish synagogue. Paul stood up and told the people how the Jewish leaders in Jerusalem had caused the death of Jesus. Then he went on to say how God had raised Jesus from the dead. Now, in the name of Jesus they could be saved from their sins.

As they left the synagogue many of the Jews asked the apostles to come back the next Sabbath. When that day came there were many people at the synagogue to hear them. But the Jewish leaders were angry with this new teaching about Jesus. They spoke against Paul and Barnabas. Then Paul stood up.

'God sent us first to you Jews', he said, 'to preach his word to you. But, as you will not hear us, then we shall turn to the Gentiles.'

The Gentiles (foreigners) were glad when they heard this, and many of them became followers of Jesus. But in their anger the leading Jews stirred up many of the people of the city against the apostles. Paul and Barnabas were driven out of Antioch. They made their way to Iconium (*Eye-cone-i-um*), and for some time they preached to the people there.

But their enemies had come after them from Antioch and again they stirred up the people. As they were in great danger of being stoned the apostles fled for their lives, to the town of Lystra (*List-ra*). Here they saw a man who had been lame from birth. Paul went up to him and spoke.

'Stand up on your feet,' he said.

When the man did this all the people were amazed.

'The gods have come down to us in the form of men,' they shouted.

The priest of the heathen temple came out with oxen ready to make a sacrifice to these 'gods'. But Paul cried out in horror, saying that they were only men and not gods at all.

At this moment the Jews from Antioch and Iconium came up

The people stoned Paul and left him for dead.

and once more roused the people, who stoned Paul and left him for dead outside the gates of the city. But even as the others stood round him, he rose to his feet and went back into the city. Next day they went on to Derbe (*Der-bee*), where they preached and made other disciples.

The time had come for them to return home. The apostles turned back and went once more to the towns they had visited. In each town they left elders in charge of the little groups of disciples. So they made their way back to the sea coast. From there they sailed back to Antioch, where their missionary journey had begun many months before.

Your turn now...

Research and writing

Use this chapter as a guide, and read Acts, Chapters 13 and 14. Then write out what you think Paul might have written in his diary for this period.

Investigation

Read Acts, Chapter 13, verses 14 and 51; Acts, Chapter 14, verses 6 and 25. Which towns were visited by the apostles on this journey? Look at your map and, using the scale, work out how far they travelled.

Research and discussion

Discuss the following with your friends and teacher.
a) Why did the leading Jews stir up a persecution against Paul and Barnabas?
b) Which of the following words do you think describe the actions of the apostles' enemies:
    merciful   jealous   understanding   cruel   fearful?

16

Paul sets out for Europe

For some time Paul and Barnabas stayed in Antioch. Then, one day, Paul said to Barnabas:

'Let us go back again to the towns we visited on our journey, and see the people there.'

Barnabas wanted to take his nephew, John Mark, once more. But Paul would not hear of this because he had left them on their last journey. After a great deal of argument, the two friends parted. Barnabas took Mark with him to Cyprus, but Paul chose a new friend, a man named Silas (*Sigh-lass*).

This time Paul and his friend went overland until they came to Derbe and then to Lystra. Here there lived a young man named Timothy, and Paul chose him to go with them. On they went to Iconium. At each town they met the men and women

'Come over to Macedonia and help us.'

who had become followers of Jesus on their first journey.

From Iconium Paul and Silas set out for the north. But they soon felt in their hearts that God did not want them to go that way. For some time they made their way to the west, and they felt again that God was holding them back. But at last God led them to the sea coast and to a town called Troas (*Tro-az*): this is the Troy of our history books.

That night Paul had a strange dream. In it he saw a man from Macedonia (*Massy-doe-ni-a*) calling to him.

'Come over to Macedonia,' he said, 'and help us.'

Paul knew that this was a sign from God. He and his friends set off right away across the sea. This was a great day. For the first time Paul was taking the word of God from Asia into Europe.

The man of Paul's dream may well have been the man who later wrote the book of the Acts of the Apostles. He was a doctor named Luke, and he was probably a Greek. When we read this story in the Bible we may see that the writer often uses the word 'we' showing that he was with Paul and Silas on their journey.

Paul would be glad to have a doctor like Luke with him. Paul was not a very strong man and he was often ill.

From Troas the apostles sailed to Macedonia and made their way to the city of Philippi (*Filly-pie*). For some days they stayed there teaching. As on Paul's first journey people began to follow Jesus. But once again there was to be trouble for the apostles. We shall read about this in the next chapter.

Your turn now...

Research and writing

Answer each of the following questions with a sentence.
a) Why do you think Paul wished to revisit the towns of his first journey?
b) Why did Paul and Barnabas argue?
c) What was the result of their argument?

Investigation

Look at the map of Paul's second journey. How far did he and his friends travel this time?
What sort of difficulties did such a journey present?

Research and discussion

Discuss the following with your friends and teacher.
a) What sort of preparations would such a journey require?
b) What kind of men would undertake such a mission?
c) What rewards did they get from the journey?

Map of Paul's second missionary journey.

17

Paul and Silas in Prison

It was the Sabbath day in Philippi. Paul and his friends were going to pray and they were followed by a strange girl. She seemed to have the gift of seeing into the future. From this her masters were able to make quite a lot of money. All at once the girl began to shout after Paul and Silas.

'These men are the servants of the Most High God,' she cried. 'They will teach you the way of life.'

This went on for many days. Then, at last, Paul grew angry and turned to the girl.

'You evil spirit,' he said, 'in the name of Jesus, come out of her.'

At that very moment the girl was freed from her evil spirit. Her masters were very angry, for she could no longer earn money for them. They stirred up the crowd and Paul and Silas were seized and taken to the magistrates. Their cloaks were torn from their backs and they were beaten with canes. Then they were thrown into prison.

The keeper of the prison was told to guard them well. He put them inside a cell and locked their feet in the stocks. There, in the night, Paul and Silas sang hymns of praise to God, while the other prisoners listened to them.

All at once there was a great earthquake. The whole prison was shaken and the doors flew open. Every one of the prisoners found that he was free. The keeper of the prison awoke from sleep in fear. He saw the doors open and thought that all the prisoners must have gone. He would have to answer for them with his life. So he drew his sword to kill himself.

'Do not harm yourself,' cried Paul, 'for we are all here.'

The jailor fell down in front of Paul and Silas.

'What must I do to be saved?' he asked.

'Believe in the Lord Jesus Christ,' he was told, 'and you and your family will be saved.'

The cell where Paul and Silas were imprisoned.

Then the apostles told him all about Jesus. The man took them and bathed their backs, where they had been beaten. Then he gave them food. He and all his family were baptised.

The next day word came from the magistrates that Paul and Silas were to be set free. But Paul would not go. He was a Roman citizen who had been beaten without trial, and thrown into prison. This was against the law. The magistrates must come themselves to set him free.

The magistrates were afraid and soon came to the prison. They asked Paul and Silas to go away quietly. The two apostles went back to meet those who had become followers of Jesus in Philippi. Then they left the city to go to other parts.

Your turn now...

Research and writing

Answer each of the following questions with a sentence.
a) What was the girl like who met Paul and his friends?
b) What did she shout after Paul and Silas?
c) What did Paul do?

Discussion

Discuss with your friends and teacher why you think the girl's masters were angry.

Illustration

Draw a picture of Paul and Silas in their prison cell. Pay careful attention to their feet.

Drama

With your friends write out and act a detailed play. Start with Paul and Silas being taken before the magistrate and end with the two apostles leaving the city.

18

The Unknown God

When Paul and his little party left Philippi they made their way to other towns. When they told the people about Jesus there were always some who believed. But many of the Jews were angry and caused trouble. Sometimes there were riots and the apostles had to flee. But their enemies followed them and there was often great danger for Paul and his friends. There was danger, too, for anyone who helped them. The house of one, Jason, was raided by men trying to find Paul and Silas, and Jason and some of his friends were dragged before the rulers of the city.

At last Paul went on to Athens, leaving Silas and Timothy behind. To Paul it seemed that the city of Athens was full of

The altar to the unknown god.

idols. The people of the city had many gods to worship. Paul went to the synagogue and preached to the Jews. He spoke to the crowds in the market place.

The Greeks were eager to hear any new teaching and they loved to argue. So they brought Paul to one of the hills of Athens where meetings were often held. Paul stood up in their midst.

'Men of Athens,' he said, 'you are superstitious people. As I looked at all your idols and your temples I saw a strange thing. I saw an altar to an unknown god. This God, whom you worship but do not know, he is the God of whom I tell you.'

Paul went on to tell them how God was the maker of the earth and all that is in it.

'You cannot keep such a God in your temples,' said Paul. 'He is not made of gold, or silver, or stone.'

Then Paul told them the story of Jesus, and how God had raised him from the dead. Many people laughed at these words. How could anyone come back from the dead? But there were some who believed.

Paul did not stay long at Athens. He moved on to Corinth. There he stayed with a man and his wife who were tentmakers. Paul himself had learned this trade as a boy, so he was able to help them and earn his own keep.

Each Sabbath Paul went to the synagogue to talk to the Jews. He also told the Greeks about Jesus. It was not long before he was joined by Silas and Timothy. But many of the Jews would not listen to his words. Paul made up his mind that he would no longer preach to the Jews: he would turn to the Gentiles instead.

For many months Paul stayed in Corinth. Many people became Christians as they heard his words. The Jews from the synagogue tried to stop Paul and took him before the ruler. But the ruler would have nothing to do with them.

At last Paul left his many friends in Corinth. He sailed back to Asia and stayed for a time at Ephesus (*Eff-es-us*). The Jews to whom he spoke wanted him to stay, but Paul wanted to go home. After making a promise to come back to Ephesus he set sail for home, calling at Jerusalem before going back to Antioch once more.

Your turn now...

Research and writing

The following words are all used in this chapter. Write a sentence about each: Athens   Jason   altar   idols   tentmakers.

Discussion

With your friends and teacher discuss the following points.
a) Paul encouraged riots.
b) Paul's friends were often in danger.
c) The Athenians laughed at Paul's story of the Resurrection.
d) After visiting Ephesus, Paul was tired and wanted to go home.

Illustration

Draw a picture of Paul talking to the Athenians on the hill.
   Try to capture the excitement as Paul and the Athenians argued about the points he made.

19

A Riot at Ephesus

For some time Paul remained at Antioch. Then he set off on his third missionary journey. He went overland from Antioch, to visit once more the towns of Derbe, Lystra, Iconium and the other Antioch. Then, as he had promised, he went back to Ephesus.

For more than two years Paul stayed in the city, teaching both Jews and Gentiles about Jesus. Many people were healed, some of them without even seeing Paul. To some Paul sent something of his own, such as a handkerchief. When this was brought to the sick person he was healed at once. This may sound strange, but these objects gave people great faith when they knew that Paul had sent them.

In Ephesus there were many people who believed in magic. When they heard Paul speak some of these became followers of Jesus. They even brought out their books of magic into the streets and burnt them in public. So the word of Jesus spread in and around the city.

But in Ephesus there was a great temple to the goddess Diana. Inside there was an image of the goddess. It was said to have fallen from heaven. Pilgrims from far and near came to Ephesus to worship at the temple of Diana. Many of these pilgrims used to buy little silver images of Diana and the temple to take home with them.

The men who made the images were afraid that the teaching of Paul was going to harm their trade. Paul had said that there were no gods made by human hands. If people believed this they would no longer buy their images. The silversmiths were so angry that they went out into the city.

'Great is Diana of the Ephesians!' they cried in the streets.

Soon the whole city was in an uproar. Two of Paul's friends

Map of Paul's third missionary journey.

were seized. Paul wanted to go out and speak to the people, but he was kept away by other disciples who feared for his life. For two hours there was shouting and rioting.

Then, at last, the Town Clerk came on the scene. He told the angry crowd that they were breaking the law by this riot. If the Romans were to hear of it they might punish the city. If the silversmiths had any complaint against Paul then they must take it to the court.

At last the people came to their senses. They went home quietly. Paul had some words to say to the disciples in the city. Then he set out on his travels once more. He was going to Macedonia and Greece.

Your turn now...

Research and writing

1 Answer the following questions about Paul's third missionary journey.
   a) Which town was the starting point for his journey?
   b) Which towns did he visit before going to Ephesus?
   c) Using the scale given on the map, how far is it from Paul's starting point to Ephesus?

2 Imagine you are Paul starting on this third journey. Keep a diary of the places visited and what happened there. Make the diary more interesting by using your imagination and writing about everyday occurrences which might have happened.

Discussion

Discuss wth your friends and teacher why the silversmiths in Ephesus were afraid of Paul's teaching. What was the outcome of their fear?

You will find reading Acts, Chapter 19, verses 24–41 helpful here.

— 20 —

Paul heals a Boy

From Ephesus Paul went to visit the Christians in Macedonia and Greece. When, at last, he came to Corinth, he found that he had many enemies there and a plot was made to kill him. His friends went down to the sea to find a boat. But Paul decided that it was safer to go back by land. In this way he could escape from his enemies. So he set out once more for the north and came to Philippi. From here he sailed to Troas and met his friends who had sailed from Corinth.

On the first day of the week Paul and his friends met together in an upstairs room. They had met to take bread and wine in memory of Jesus, and to hear Paul speak to them. There was a boy with them who was sitting on the window-sill. As Paul spoke for a very long time the boy grew drowsy. At last he fell asleep. All at once, to the horror of those in the room, he fell out of the window.

Paul hurried down to the ground, where the boy lay still as if dead. But Paul took him in his arms and turned to those who stood around.

'Do not worry,' he said, 'the boy is alive.'

They were very glad to hear these cheering words. They went back upstairs and all night long they listened to Paul speak. The next day he left them to join his friends not far from Troas.

Paul and his party made their way down the coast in a small ship. Each night they put in at a small port until the next day. At last they came to Miletus (*My-lee-tus*), where they were not

There was a boy sitting on the window-sill.

very far from Ephesus. But Paul did not want to visit this city again. He was keen to get to Jerusalem in time for the Feast of Pentecost.

So Paul sent for the leaders of the Church at Ephesus and they came to meet him. When they heard that he was going to Jerusalem they were afraid for him. They knew the danger he would have to face from those Jews who would try to kill him. There were many such Jews at Jerusalem. With great sadness they parted, and Paul's ship made its way along the coast until it came to Patara (*Pat-a-ra*).

Here a large ship was found to take them over the open sea to Tyre. Later, when he was at Caesarea, many of Paul's friends tried to stop him from going to Jerusalem. One of them, a prophet, told him that the Jews of the city would take Paul and hand him over to the Romans.

'Why do you weep and make me sad?' asked Paul. 'I am ready to face my enemies and even to die at Jerusalem for the sake of Jesus.'

So the little party, with Paul at its head, made its way to the great city of Jerusalem. The disciples in the city were very pleased to see them all.

Your turn now...

Research and writing

1 Continue writing the diary for Paul's third journey. Note the places visited, events which took place, and people he met. Finish this diary entry by stating how many miles were travelled from Ephesus to Jerusalem.

2 Read Acts, Chapter 20, verse 16 and Chapter 21, verses 8–14. Next, rewrite the following sentences, putting in the missing words as you do so.
  a) A friend of Paul's, who was a prophet in _____, warned him of the Jews in Jerusalem.
  b) 'I am ready to face my _____ and even to die at _____ for the sake of _____,' said Paul.
  c) Paul wished to be in Jerusalem in time for the Feast of _____.

Drama

With some friends act out the scene concerning Paul and his friends and the drowsy boy. (Acts, Chapter 20, verses 7–12.)

—— 21 ——
Paul meets his Enemies in the Temple

When Paul came to Jerusalem the apostles and disciples were eager to hear all that he had to tell them about his missionary journeys. When he told them that he had turned from the Jews to preach to the Gentiles his friends were worried. They warned Paul that he had many enemies in the city because of his work among the Gentiles. Some of his enemies came from as far away as Asia Minor, where Paul had done much of his teaching. These Jews would soon hear that Paul was in Jerusalem, and would try to kill him.

One day the Jews from Asia saw Paul in the Temple. They took hold of him and shouted to others to help them.

'This is the man who teaches against the Law and the Temple,' they cried. 'He even brought Gentiles into the Temple.'

This was not true, for Paul had only been seen with a Greek in the city. But the people in the crowd were very angry. Paul was dragged from the Temple and the Jews tried to kill him. They would have done so if the Romans had not heard what was going on. The soldiers ran quickly from their castle next to the Temple and the Jews stopped beating Paul.

The Roman captain took Paul and had him bound in chains. With all the shouting he could not hear what was the reason for the uproar. Paul was taken into the castle. The soldiers had to carry him to avoid the angry crowd which pressed about them.

Then Paul asked the captain if he could speak to the people. From the stairs leading to the castle he cried out to the Jews. All listened quietly as he spoke to them. He told them how he had at first persecuted the Christian Church. Then he told them how he had been blinded when Jesus spoke to him on the road to Damascus. Then he spoke of his work among the Jews and the Gentiles. When he told them that the Lord had sent him to the

From the steps Paul spoke to the Jews.

Gentiles the crowd grew angry again.

Once more the captain had to take Paul into the castle for safety. He was tied up, and as he was led away the captain gave orders that he must be beaten to find out the reason for the riot. But Paul spoke to the centurion.

'Does the law allow you to flog a Roman,' he asked, 'when he has not been tried?'

When the captain heard that Paul was a Roman he was afraid, for it was he who had ordered Paul to be put in chains. By Roman law no man could be flogged unless guilty. No Roman could be flogged at all.

Your turn now...

Research and writing

Read Acts, Chapter 21, verses 27–36. Next, answer the following questions in sentences.
a) Why were Paul's enemies so angry with him?
b) How was Paul rescued from the Temple?
c) What did Paul say to the Jews from the castle steps?

Illustration

Draw Paul being led away to be flogged. Try to capture the tense atmosphere in your drawing.

Discussion

Discuss with your friends and teacher why Paul was not flogged. Do you think this was a just law? (Acts, Chapter 22, verses 27–29.)

22

Paul in a Roman Prison

After the Romans had saved Paul from his own people in the Temple, Paul spent the night in the Roman castle. The next day the Roman captain brought him before the Chief Priest and the Council. He wanted to hear what Paul had done to make the Jews so angry.

We may remember that Paul had been a Pharisee before he had become a follower of Jesus. This caused some trouble in the Council. Some of its members were Pharisees, and they did not agree with the others. There was a great deal of argument and many angry words were spoken. The Roman captain was afraid that at any moment Paul would be seized and killed. Once again he took him away to the safety of the castle.

That night, as Paul lay in his cell, he had a wonderful vision. He had often dreamt of going to Rome to carry the word of God to that great city. Now, in the night, Jesus stood at his side and spoke to him.

'You have spoken to the people of Jerusalem about me,' said

The captain listened to the boy's story.

Jesus. 'Now you must go and speak of me in Rome.'

The next day some of the Jews plotted to kill Paul. They made a vow that they would not eat until this had been done. Their plan was to lie in wait for Paul and to catch him when the Romans brought him to the priests again for trial.

But Paul's young nephew heard about the plot. He came to the Roman castle to see Paul, and the soldiers let him in. Paul heard the boy's story and then he sent him to the Roman captain. The captain listened to the boy. Then he sent him away and told him to say nothing to anyone about what he had heard.

The captain called together a large band of soldiers. They were to take Paul away to Caesarea, to the Roman Governor there. He would then be safe from his enemies. Both foot soldiers and horsemen set out that night, with Paul in their midst. When they had gone a safe distance, the men on foot came back to the castle. The horsemen rode on with Paul to Caesarea.

A few days later the Chief Priest and some of his men came from Jerusalem. They had come to Caesarea to accuse Paul of many things. They told Felix (*Fee-lix*), the Governor, that Paul had caused riots among the Jews in many places. They said that he was the leader of a new religion, and had spoken against their holy Temple.

When Felix had heard these words he turned to Paul and asked him to speak. Of course, Paul said that he had not stirred up the people. He agreed that he was a follower of the new religion, called the Way, but he was also a good Jew and obeyed the Law.

Felix could find nothing against Paul. But he wanted to hear what the captain had to say, who had sent Paul to him. So Paul was kept in charge of a Roman officer, but he was allowed to see his friends.

From time to time Felix sent for Paul to hear what he had to say about Jesus. He hoped that Paul might give him bribes to set him free. This went on for two years. Then Felix went back to Rome and a new Governor took his place.

Your turn now...

Research and writing

Read the chapter again carefully. Then read Acts, Chapter 23, verses 6–11; and Acts, Chapter 24, verse 24.

a) Put each of the following words into a sentence to show its meaning: Pharisees   imprisoned   vision. Use a dictionary where necessary.

b) Write a sentence about each of the following people: Ananias   Felix   Drusilla.

Drama

With your friends, prepare and write a detailed drama of the events of this chapter.
Start with the plot to kill Paul and end with his being brought before Felix.

Illustration

Choose an incident from this chapter and draw it as vividly as you can.

23
Paul on Trial

The name of the new Governor was Festus. When he was in Jerusalem the Jews tried to make him bring Paul to the city for trial. They hoped that Festus would agree to do this. Then they could kill Paul when he was on his way. But Festus was going to Caesarea and he told the Jews that they could accuse Paul there.

Some days later Festus came to Caesarea and called Paul for trial. Once again the Jews were there to accuse him. But once again they were not able to prove anything against Paul. Then Festus, trying to please the Jews, spoke to Paul.

'Will you go up to Jerusalem, to be tried by me there?' he asked.

'I am being tried by Romans,' said Paul. 'This is right, for I am a Roman citizen. I have done no wrong to the Jews. If what they say about me is false, then no one can hand me over to the Jews. I appeal to the Emperor.'

Paul had every right to appeal to Caesar, for he was a Roman

'I appeal to the Emperor.'

citizen. But once he had done this there was only one thing that Festus could do. Paul had appealed to Caesar and to Caesar he must go. This, of course, meant a journey to Rome. Paul must have thought about the words that Jesus had said to him one night:

'You must go and speak of me in Rome.'

About this time King Herod Agrippa was at Caesarea for a few days. When Festus told him about Paul, who had been there so long, the king said that he would like to see him. So Paul was brought before Festus and Agrippa. The king asked Paul to tell him about himself. This Paul did. He told how he had been brought up, and of his meeting with Jesus on the road to Damascus. Then he spoke of his preaching, first to the Jews and then to the Gentiles. For this, he told the king, the Jews had seized him in the Temple, and had even tried to kill him.

Paul went on to say that he had done nothing wrong. He had only told the Jews what Moses and the prophets had said would happen. The king was struck by Paul and what he had said.

'You almost persuade me to be a Christian,' said Agrippa.

After this, as the king and Festus spoke together, they agreed that Paul had done nothing wrong. He did not deserve to die, or even to be put in prison. If he had not made his appeal to Caesar he might have been set free at once. But this was not possible now: he must go to Rome, to the Emperor.

Your turn now...

Research and writing

1 Answer the following questions in sentences.
   a) Who was to judge Paul?
   b) Were the Jews' charges proved?
   c) Why did Paul refuse to go to Jerusalem and to whom did he appeal?

2 In your own words say what you think Paul said to Agrippa.

Drama

With your friends act out the story of Paul being brought before Festus and Agrippa. Include Bernice (Acts, Chapter 25, verse 23) in your drama and end with Agrippa's words to Festus (Acts, Chapter 26, verse 32).

24

The Voyage to Rome

The time came for Paul to be taken to Rome. He and other prisoners were put under the care of a Roman centurion. They set sail from Caesarea in a ship that would take them along the coast to Myra, where they could find another ship to take them to Rome. On the next day the ship came to Sidon (*Sigh-don*). Here the centurion was very kind to Paul and let him visit some friends. Then they put out to sea once more.

The winds were against them, but at last the ship came to Myra, in what we now call Asia Minor. Here they found a large grain ship that was sailing from Alexandria in Egypt to Rome. The centurion took his soldiers and prisoners on board and the ship set sail.

For many days the ship made little headway against the strong winds. When they reached Crete a harbour was found. Here they could shelter from the wind and waves. But the

The ship in which Paul sailed for Rome.

longer they spent there, the more dangerous the voyage would be. Already it was late in the year. The time for sailing was almost past. When winter came very few ships risked the open sea.

Paul spoke to the centurion and the captain of the ship. He told them that it would not be wise to try to go to Rome. But the captain said that the harbour was not a good place to spend the winter. He wanted to sail round the island to Phenice (*Fee-nice-ee*), and stay there. This port is also called Phoenix (*Fee-nix*).

On a day of gentle winds they set off to sail along the coast of the island. Then, all at once, a great storm blew up. The wind filled the sails of the ship. Nothing could be done. The only safe thing was for the ship to run before the wind.

The sailors were very much afraid for the ship, for the wind was so strong. To help make the ship safer they put thick ropes round the hull. This was done as the ship went along, then the ropes were pulled tight to hold the planks together. Huge waves beat the sides of the ship and the sailors began to throw some of the cargo into the sea. Even some of the ship's tackle went over the side.

For many days the storm blew. The sky was filled with dark clouds. The sailors were lost for there was nothing to steer by. There was no sun in the day, no stars at night. It was not long before those on board began to give up hope of being saved. But then Paul stood up in their midst.

'Be brave,' he said. 'The ship will be lost, but no one will die. An angel of God has come to me and told me that all of us will be saved. We shall be cast up on an island.'

How God kept his promise to save them all we shall read in the next chapter.

Your turn now...

Discussion

Storms can be dangerous and frightening. Discuss with your friends and teacher any storm which you have experienced.

What were you most afraid of? What happened during the storm? What happened afterwards?

Research and writing

Finish each of the following sentences by rewriting it with the

missing word or words included.
a) The ship's captain wanted to sail his vessel to _____.
b) The sailors decided to throw _____.
c) As the sun or stars could not be seen the sailors could not _____.
d) Paul said _____.

Illustration

Draw a dramatic scene from the story.

— 25 —

The Shipwreck

For fourteen days Paul's ship was blown to and fro by the storm. Then, one night, the sailors knew that they were near to some land. They had no idea where it was, and in the night nothing could be seen. Anchors were put out to keep the ship steady all night. Then they waited in fear for the day.

Some of the sailors had made up their minds to escape from the ship. They began to let down the small boat off the deck. Paul saw what they were doing and spoke to the centurion. The sailors had to be stopped. Their help would be needed to rescue those on board. The soldiers drew their swords and cut the ropes that held the small boat. Quickly it slid away out of sight.

When day came Paul was very calm. He told those on board that they must eat some food. They needed this to keep up their strength. He himself took some bread, gave thanks to God, and gave it to them. Then they began to throw out the wheat from the hold. This was to lighten the ship and give a better chance of escape.

In the light of day a beach could be seen. The sailors let go the anchors that had held the ship during the night. A sail was hoisted and they tried to drive the ship up on the beach. But before they got there the ship ran aground on a sand bank. The bow stuck fast and the stern began to break up under the heavy waves.

When the soldiers saw this they wanted to kill the prisoners. The Romans would have to answer for them with their lives.

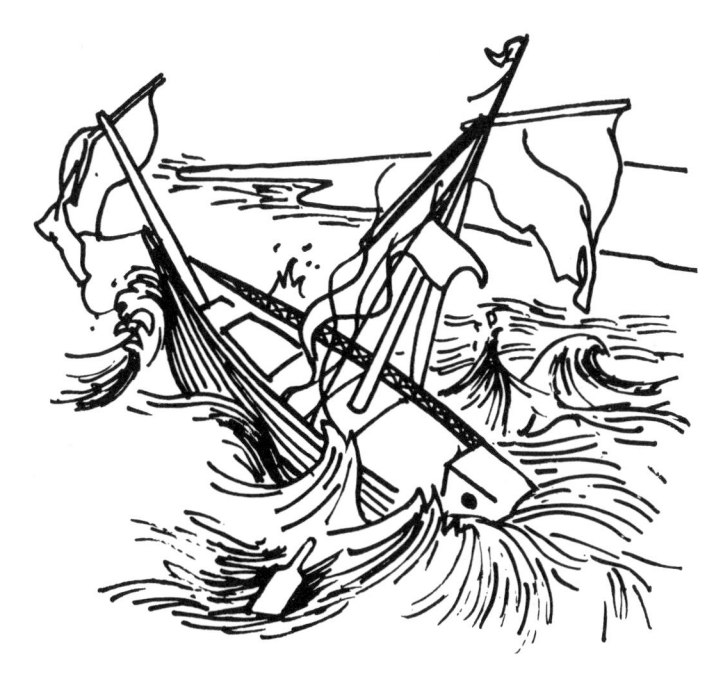

The bow stuck fast and the stern began to break up.

Now it seemed that the prisoners might swim away and escape. But the centurion wanted to save Paul. He stopped his men from killing the others. The he gave the orders for those who could swim to make their way to the land. The others were to follow, helped by bits of wood and planks from the ship. Soon everyone reached the shore in safety.

The place where they landed was the island of Melita (*Mellyta*), today we call it Malta. Many of the people came down to the shore to help. A fire was lit to warm the wet, cold men from the ship. Paul himself went to gather some sticks for the fire. As he did so a viper came out and wrapped itself round his hand.

When the men of the island saw this they thought that Paul must be an evil man. Perhaps he was a murderer. He had been saved from the sea but now justice was to be done. He would die from the bite of the snake. Paul was very calm. He shook the viper from his hand into the fire. Each moment those who stood around waited for him to fall dead from its bite. But when they saw that all was well they made up their minds that Paul was not an evil man. He must be a god.

Near to the spot where Paul and the others had been saved was the home of the chief man of the island, called Publius. He took the men from the ship to his home. For three days he looked after them there.

At this time the father of Publius was ill. Paul went to him, prayed, and healed him. Soon the news of this miracle spread round the island. Those who were sick came or were carried to Paul. He healed them all. So the days of winter went by. At last the time came to continue the voyage to Rome.

Your turn now...

Research and discussion

In dangerous and frightening situations it is easy to panic. Discuss with your friends and teacher how Paul's behaviour affected those around him during the shipwreck.

Writing

1 Put the following words into sentences to show what they mean: Malta   viper   Publius.

2 Answer each of the following questions with a sentence.
  a) Why did the soldiers want to kill the prisoners?
  b) Who was in charge of the soldiers?
  c) What was Paul doing when the viper wrapped itself round his hand?
  d) What did the onlookers think when they saw the viper on Paul's hand?
  e) Where was Paul going to travel on to?

— 26 —

Paul's Last Days in Rome

For three months the Romans and their prisoners stayed on the island of Malta. Then they found a ship that had spent the winter there. They set sail for Italy once more. The people of Malta were very kind to them. They gave them food and clothes and all that they needed to take with them.

The voyage to Italy was calm, and in a few days they came to Puteoli (*Pew-tee-o-lie*). Here they stayed for a week before making their way overland to Rome.

Map of Paul's journey to Rome.

At last Paul came to the great city that he had so longed to see. He came, not as a free man, but as a prisoner. But being a Roman citizen and not having been found guilty, he was treated well. He was allowed to live in his own house, but always with a Roman soldier to guard him.

In Rome, as in all large cities, there were many Jews. Paul called them to meet him and he told them why he was in Rome. He told them all that had happened on his missionary journeys and in Jerusalem. These Jews had heard of this new religion, the Way. They knew that the Jews of Jerusalem and other towns were against it. But they wanted to hear what Paul had to say.

When they heard Paul speak there were some who believed what he had said, but others did not. It was the same old story: many Jews refused the word of Jesus. Once more Paul was to preach the name of Jesus to the Gentiles.

For two years Paul lived there, in his own house, with the soldier who was his guard. Many people came to his house to learn of Jesus. Many of them became members of the Christian Church of Rome.

The end of Paul's story is not to be found in the Acts of the Apostles. It seems that he was allowed to leave Rome and was then brought back a second time. It was then that his life came to a tragic end.

One night a great fire broke out in Rome. A large part of the city was burnt. Word spread that the Christians had done it. Many people think that it was Nero, the cruel Roman Emperor, who started this story.

Hundreds of Christians were put to death in cruel ways. Some were burnt, some thrown to the lions, and some crucified. Many of them died in the Circus, or arena, in front of crowds of cheering Romans.

Both Paul and Peter were in Rome at this time. Both died for their faith. It is said that Peter was crucified upside down. This was because he did not think himself worthy of dying as his Master, Jesus, had done. Paul was a Roman and he died a Roman death, by the sword. He was beheaded a short way from the city.

So the life of the first great Christian missionary came to an end. But his work lived on after him. The faith that he had brought to Rome was to spread through the Roman Empire. In the next few chapters we shall read about some of the letters that Paul wrote to the early Christians. We can find twenty-one letters in our New Testament, written by Paul and other apostles.

Your turn now...

Research and writing

Read the passage again carefully. Next read Acts, Chapter 28, verses 11–16; and verses 30–31.
Now answer the following.
a) Describe in your own words Paul's journey from Malta to Rome.
b) Name the boat he sailed in and the places he visited.
c) Say how long Paul lived in Rome and what he did during this time.
d) Say how and why Paul died.

Drama

Act out the following scenes with some of your friends. Check the passage for background details:
a) the departure from Malta;
b) Paul talking to visitors in his house in Rome.

27

Christian Behaviour

In the towns visited by Paul and his friends small groups of Christians met together. They often needed help and advice about their new religion, but Paul could not always be there to give it. Travel in those days was so slow that Paul could not have visited the towns very often. Sometimes, too, he was in prison. But even if he could not go, he could send letters. Some of these letters from Paul to the new churches have been found. They are called Epistles, the Greek word for letters. We can read them in our New Testament.

Letters were written by other apostles, too, men like Peter, James and John. Often they are very hard to understand. But

Small things that do important work.

there are some parts that we must read. The next few chapters are about some of the advice that Paul sent in his letters.

One of the most important things that Paul had to say was about how Christians ought to live. In his letter to the Romans he said that our bodies belong to God. We must always work and live for him. But Paul knew that this was not easy, even for a man like him.

'I want to do good things,' he said in his letter, 'but I don't do them. I try not to do bad things and find myself doing them. But there is someone who can help us, Jesus Christ our Lord.'

In some of his letters Paul spoke of the Christian Church as the body of Christ. Our bodies have many parts, each with its own work to do. The members of the Church are like parts of Christ's body. Each has his own work to do for God. Some are called by God to preach or teach. Some he calls to heal or to help others.

James, too, has something to say in his letter about a part of the body. It is the tongue. It is only a tiny part, but what a lot it can do. People have to be very careful to control their tongues. They can do much good, but they can also do great harm.

When we read this part of James's letter we find other small things that are very important. When the rider puts a bit in the mouth of his horse he can make him go where he wants. The rudder of a great ship is only small, but the steersman can use it to make the ship go where he wishes. Ships today are very much bigger than those James saw, but what he said in his letter is still true. So is what he said about fire. How big a fire can start from a tiny spark. We all know how true this is.

People never found it easy to do what Jesus told them. Paul's teaching was no easier. In many ways it reminds us of the teaching of Jesus. If we read Romans, Chapter 12, we find some words of Paul that remind us of the words of Jesus in the Sermon on the Mount.

'Be glad with those who are happy, and be sad with those who are sad,' wrote Paul. 'Do not be proud or think that you are wiser than others. Never pay back evil for evil. Be good to those who do you wrong. If your enemy is hungry feed him. If he is thirsty give him a drink.'

Your turn now...

Reading, research and writing

Read the chapter again carefully. Next read James, Chapter 3, verses 3–5.

1 Make a list of other small things which do important work. Say what this work is and add illustrations if you wish.

2 Read Romans, Chapter 7, verse 19.
   a) Write the meaning of this verse in your own words.
   b) Do you think this ever applied to you, or to other people? Write down your opinions about this.

3 Read Romans, Chapter 12, verses 17 and 20; Matthew, Chapter 5, verses 39–46. Write down in your own words a comparison between the teaching of Jesus and the teaching of Paul.

Drama

With your friends work out a drama where a 'small thing' is important in saving a life or lives.

28

Christian Love

In his teaching Jesus often told his followers that they must love one another. He also told them to love their enemies. The apostles often said the same thing in their teaching and in their letters. In one of his letters John wrote these words:

'Let us love one another, for love comes from God. A man who does not love cannot know God, for God himself is love.'

Then John went on to say how God had shown his love for men by sending his own Son, Jesus Christ, into the world.

One of the best known and best loved chapters in the Bible is in a letter of Paul. It is part of the first letter he wrote to the Christians at Corinth. Chapter 13 of this letter is often called Paul's 'Hymn of Love'. Where some Bibles use the word 'charity' this means, of course, the same as love.

GOD SO LOVED THE WORLD

'God so loved the world.'

When Paul began this part of his letter he may have been thinking about the work he and the apostles did for God. God had called men to preach and teach for him. He might even ask them to die for him, as Jesus himself had done. Stephen and James, and perhaps many others, had died for their faith. Whatever God asked them to do, Paul wrote in his letter, they must have love.

'It does not matter how well I speak,' he wrote. 'If I have no love I am just like a noisy instrument. I may have great knowledge and great faith, but if I have no love, I am nothing. I may give all that I have to the poor. Even if I give up my body to be burnt, without love it means nothing at all.

'Those who are filled with love are patient and kind. They are never boastful, proud, rude, or selfish. Love has no limits; it can do anything. Faith, hope and love are three things that last for ever. But the greatest of these three is love.'

As well as his words about love, Paul wrote about faith and

hope. We shall read about Christian Faith and Christian Hope in later chapters of this book.

Your turn now...

Reading and discussion

Read the whole of I Corinthians, Chapter 13. Now, with your friends and teacher, discuss the following.
a) What Paul writes about several things which are not worthwhile without love.
b) What Paul says about love in this chapter. Do you agree with him?
c) Your favourite verses in this chapter – and why you like them.

Writing

Write in your own words what Jesus said about love to his disciples in St John's Gospel, Chapter 15, verses 12–13.

Note

INRI – these are the first letters of four Roman words which stand for: Jesus, Nazareth, King, Jews.

— 29 —
The Christian's Armour

Sometimes Paul thought of his life and work as being like the soldier's. Just as a soldier serves his country, so a Christian serves Jesus Christ. The life of a soldier is often hard and dangerous. In Paul's day it was hard and dangerous to be a Christian.

We know how much Paul suffered, from a letter that he wrote to the Christians at Corinth. Five times he was flogged by the Jews, his own people. Three times he was beaten with rods, by the Romans. He was often in danger on both land and sea. He was stoned and shipwrecked. He was robbed and he was put in prison. Often he was cold and hungry. Both Jews and Gentiles were his enemies.

He must have thought of this when he wrote a letter from Rome. He was a prisoner there, in his own house, when he wrote

The soldier's armour.

to his young friend Timothy.

'Be ready to suffer hardship,' he wrote, 'as a good soldier of Jesus Christ. And always be ready to please the One you serve.'

Later in his letter Paul, knowing that the end of his life was very near, was able to write:

'I have fought a good fight, and have kept faith.'

Perhaps the best known words that Paul wrote about soldiers and battle are in another letter. This was also written from Rome, to the Christians at Ephesus. As he sat in his house writing, he thought of the soldier who stood there on guard. He looked at the man's armour and at his weapons. Then he thought of the Christian soldier and the battles he had to fight for Christ.

'Be strong in the name of Jesus,' he wrote. 'Put on the armour of God. Then you will be able to fight against the devil. For our battle is not against men: it is against all kinds of evil in the world.'

Then Paul wrote about each piece of armour, and the shield the soldier carried.

'Put on the belt of truth and the breastplate of goodness. Put on the sandals of the gospel of peace. Your shield is the shield of faith, and your helmet is salvation.'

All these would help the Christian in his battle for Christ. But armour was not enough. The soldier in front of him had a spear and a sword. The Christian too, must have his weapon. His sword, said Paul, was the word of God.

But even this was not all. To be a good soldier for Christ a man must watch and pray at all times. Only then would he be able to fight against the enemies of Christ.

Your turn now...

Reading, research and writing

Read 2 Corinthians, Chapter 11, verse 24–27. Now write in your own words all that Paul suffered and the dangers he encountered for Jesus.

Discussion

With your friends and teacher discuss the things that Paul has to say about soldiers. Do you understand what he means? Does it make sense? Do you agree with him? Consider all these points in your discussions.

Drama

With a friend mime a Roman soldier putting on his armour. Check with the drawing on page 72 to make sure you get the details correct. Bear in mind your discussion when considering the importance of each piece of equipment.

30

Christian Faith

One of the longer letters in the New Testament is that written to the Hebrews. Who these Hebrews were we do not know. But they were Jewish Christians. For a long time this letter was thought to have been written by Paul, but now most people think that someone else wrote it. Who this was no one knows. One of the best parts of this letter is about faith. The words must have been of great help to the early Christians who needed encouragement. When we read Hebrews, Chapter 11, we find many of the great names of the Old Testament. They are names that we have read in Book 1, *Stories of God's People*.

The letter tells of the faith that these men and women of old had in God, long before the days of Jesus. It starts at the time of Abel and his sacrifice to God. Then it speaks of the faith of Noah, who built an ark to save his family. Abraham had faith to leave his home and find a country promised to him by God. Then follow stories of Moses, the Prophets, Judges and Kings.

Because of their faith in God these men were able to do great

The arena where games were held.

things. Many were put in prison and ill-treated. Some died for their faith. They were a great example for the Christians. With all these to read about and Jesus himself, the Christians should be filled with faith in God.

Here the writer of the letter must have thought of something he had seen many times. He had in mind a large arena where races and games took place, in Greek and Roman days. He saw runners as they got ready for their race. They took off their long and heavy clothes, so that they could run quickly. Then each set his eyes upon the winning post and tried to reach it first. So the letter goes on:

'Let us lay aside all the things that hinder us. Let us run our race well, looking towards Jesus, who gives us our faith.'

Paul, too, must have thought of the race when he wrote to the Christians at Corinth.

'All the men in a race run hard,' he wrote, 'but only one wins the prize. They run for a prize that withers, but we run for an everlasting prize.'

The prize Paul meant was, of course, the crown of leaves that was given to the victor. In the race of life the prize was the 'crown' of life, and all could win it.

Your turn now...

Reading, research and writing

Read Hebrews, Chapter 11, verses 4–38.
a) Make a list of the great examples of faith which are spoken of in these verses.
b) What evils had to be faced for faith?

Illustration

Draw a picture of the arena where games and races were held. Write beneath your picture what the chapter says about races.

Talking

Prepare a short talk on getting ready for a race. What preparations are required? What qualities must you have to take part? How do you feel as the race gets nearer?

You might ask other people for their opinion about these things after you have given your talk.

31

Christian Hope

At the end of Paul's 'Hymn of Love', in his first letter to the Christians at Corinth, he wrote about faith, hope and love. We have read what Paul and other apostles said about faith and love. Hope was always a great thing for the Jews. The stories about the Prophets in the Old Testament show that there was always hope that God would help his people.

Now, in Paul's day, there was even greater need for hope. The early Christians were often persecuted by other Jews and by Romans. In the Old Testament the book of Daniel was written to encourage the Jews and give them hope in times of persecution by the Greeks. Now we find words that were written to encourage the Christians when they were being persecuted by the Romans.

Such words are found in the last book of the Bible. This is called the Revelation of St John. It belongs to the time of two cruel Roman Emperors, Nero and Domitian (*Doe-mish-i-an*). Many Christians were put to death for their faith. We have read how Paul and Peter were among those killed by Nero.

To give the Christians hope at such a time some wonderful words were written in the Revelation. In the last two chapters of this book there is a picture in words of a new heaven and earth, and a time of perfect freedom and happiness.

We are not sure who wrote this book. Many think that it was John the disciple, brother of James. He was not put to death for his faith, but he was sent into exile on a little island called Patmos. Perhaps it was here that he saw the visions that he wrote about in this book.

John saw a new heaven and a new earth, where there was no more sea. Most people like the sea, but to John it was his enemy. During his exile on the island, it had kept him away from the people and the land he loved. In the new world there would be no cruel thing: there would be no sea.

John gives a wonderful picture of the New Jerusalem, the holy city of God. In his vision he saw this city of strength and beauty coming down out of heaven. God, whose city it was, had come to live among men. In it there was no need for sun and moon. Its light was the glory of God. The gates of the earthly city had to be closed at night to keep out evil men. But the gates of

Aα Bβ Ωω
Alpha Beta Omega

Χριστος = Christ

☧

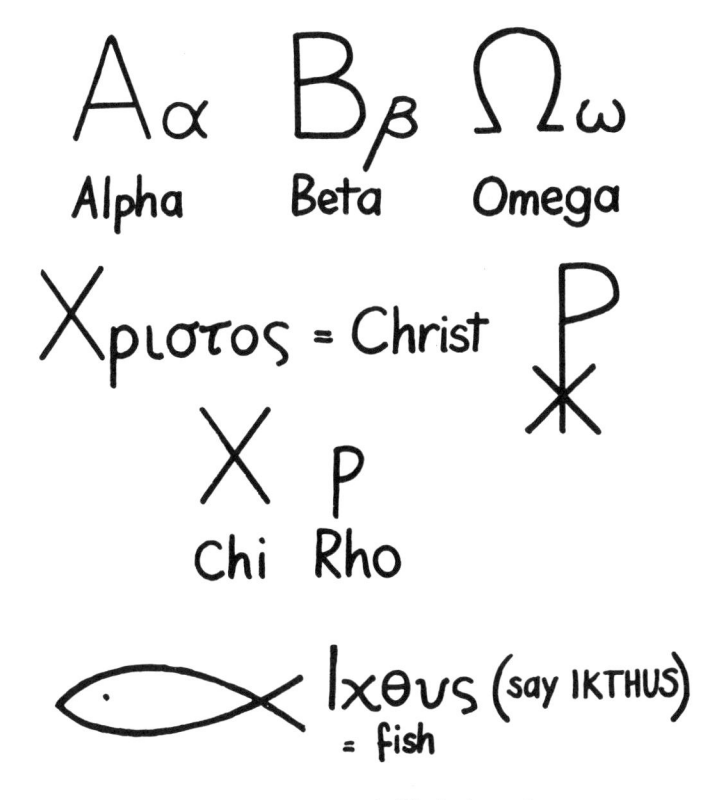

Χ Ρ
Chi Rho

Ιχθυς (say IKTHUS) = fish

Greek letters and Christian signs.

the New Jerusalem were never closed, for there was no night.

The real message of hope to the Christians was that there would be no evil in the city of God. Sorrow, pain, and death will be no more, for God has done away with them. All will be light and beauty and happiness.

For the Christians who first read this book there was often great danger. But in these words they were able to find hope. One day the city of God would be their home for ever, if they kept their faith.

Your turn now...

Research and writing

Answer the following questions in sentences.
a) Why did Christians need great hope in Paul's day?
b) Where could a Christian find words of encouragement?
c) Who wrote the book called The Revelation?

d) Who was exiled on the island of Patmos?
e) Why were the gates of earthly cities closed at night?

Discussion

1 With your friends and teacher discuss the following.
   a) What John disliked about his exile.
   b) What the disadvantages of a modern exile would be.
   c) Might there be any advantages?

2 Read about the city of God in The Revelation, Chapter 21, verse 10 to Chapter 22, verse 5. Discuss some of the advantages and disadvantages of our modern cities.

32

Christian Friendship

One of Paul's shortest letters is also one of the best. It was written when he was a prisoner in Rome. Philemon (*Fie-lee-mon*), the man to whom it was sent, lived in Colossae (*Col-oss-ee*). This city was about one hundred miles to the east of Ephesus. Philemon was a Christian and a rich man. He may have been one of the leading members of the Church in his city.

The letter is about a runaway slave who had belonged to Philemon. Slaves were quite common in those days. It seems that this slave may have stolen some of his master's goods and then fled. He came to the great city of Rome, for here he could easily hide himself.

In Rome the slave somehow met Paul and he became a Christian. Paul grew very fond of the young man, but both of them knew that he must go back to his master. Now he was a Christian the slave was ashamed of what he had done. Philemon had always treated him kindly.

Some time later, Paul sent him back to his master with a special letter to give to Philemon. He also gave him a letter to take to the other Christians in Colossae. This is, of course, Paul's Letter to the Colossians.

In his letter to Philemon Paul spoke of the slave as being his 'son', who had been 'born' to him in prison. He knew that the young man ought to be punished for what he had done. But he asked Philemon to treat him as a Christian as well as a slave.

The slave's name was Onesimus (*O-nessy-muss*). This name means 'useful'. Paul knew that he had not lived up to this name. He had been far from 'useful' to his master when he had run away. But now that he was a Christian he could put things right again.

'I know that Onesimus has not been useful to you in the past,' Paul wrote. 'But now he is useful, both to you and to me. I am sending him back to you as my son, although I should love to keep him here with me. Greet him as you would greet me, not as a slave, but as a brother.'

Paul said that he would be glad to pay back all that the slave had taken from his master, if Philemon wished it. But he also said that, in a way, Philemon owed his life to Paul. It was through Paul that Philemon had become a Christian.

'I know that you will do what I ask,' Paul wrote, 'and even more than I ask.'

We do not know what happened when Onesimus came back to Philemon. But we can be sure that they met each other as Christians, just as Paul had asked.

Your turn now...

Research and writing

1 Write at least one sentence about each of the following.
   a) Philemon;
   b) Colossae;
   c) Onesimus;
   d) Paul's letter.

2 Answer each of the following questions with a sentence.
   a) What crime had the slave committed?
   b) To which city did he flee?
   c) Why did he go there?
   d) What happened to the slave when he met Paul?
   e) How did the slave feel about his crime?

Drama

We do not know how Paul met Onesimus. Use your imagination and decide how they met. Then, with some friends, work out a play about this.

Dates of Events and the Books of the New Testament

(Many of these dates cannot be fixed with complete accuracy)

Events	A.D.	Letters	Gospels, etc.
Crucifixion of Jesus	30		
Stoning of Stephen			
Conversion of Paul	35		
	40		
1st Missionary Journey	45		
2nd Missionary Journey	50		
3rd Missionary Journey	55	↓	
Paul in prison in Caesarea			
Paul's journey to Rome	60		
Paul in prison in Rome		Letters written	
Paul and Peter martyred by Nero	65	by Paul and by	Mark
	70	other apostles	
	75	to the early	Luke
	80	Christian Churches	Matthew Acts
	85	of Asia and	
	90	Europe	
		↑	
Persecution of Christians by Domitian	95		Revelation
	100		John

— 80 —